MAN WALKING ON WATER WITH TIE ASKEW

MAN WALKING ON WATER WITH TIE ASKEW

Margaret Wilmot

The High Window

First published in the UK in 2019 by The High Window Press
3 Grovely Close
Peatmoor
Swindon
SN5 5SN
Email: abbeygatebooks@yahoo.co.uk

Designed and typeset in Palatino Linotype
by The High Window Press.
Cover Image *Man Walking on Water with Tie Askew* by Rex Ashlock
Printed and bound by Lulu.com.

In memory of my father and mother

In memory of my father and mother

CONTENTS

MAN WALKING ON WATER WITH TIE ASKEW

MY AUNT AND ZBIGNIEW HERBERT

MAN WALKING ON WATER WITH TIE ASKEW

Man Walking on Water with Tie Askew

The light was on a time-switch, flicked off
each half hour. I had to grope through
the absolute darkness of the warehouse corridor.
Then a burst of colour would take shape, become
Bicycle Woman Shrieking, or *Ochre Spot on Blue Field,*
or *Man Walking on Water with Tie Askew.*
For a week we measured and dated each canvas.
Or for a lifetime. *I'd forgotten this one,* said Dad
as a suspension bridge leapt past city towers.
Again, the light switched off.

Magic Realism on the Way Home from a Book Club on Garcia Marquez

The front door closes on the bright living-room.
Outside a milky mist veils the darkness.
Did I park in this tree?
Eucalyptus sweat sweet tears.

The reflective glow in no way emanates from my lights.
A frothing golf course is littered with giant hotels.
Huge tree-trunks parade waist-deep down the dark river.
I float through starless space for hours and hours.

A tented funfair of lights in Safeway's parking-lot signals
Christmas is coming, the goose is getting fat.

Red light. Green light.
Old children's books.
Go.

Home.
To a bright living-room where a bulky man is reading
the rug. *Look!* the man says. *Black spots.*
The rug is white. The spots are black.
See? he points. *Here.*
Here.

Here.

Childhood

The boughs of the pepper-tree were
long hair sweeping over the porch
where childhood slept in its cloud
of breath. Deer moved softly
through a world heady with scent.

There were other children then;
together in the vacant lot we found
rules for our games. The ground underfoot
was rough as we ran. Eucalyptus
clung to our shorts, our hands,

cries drifting through blue air at dusk –
while unheeded on the hour
the Campanile chimed.

August's Walking Shadows

So many have
drifted away into
their own life or death
school-mates, old flame
the colleague who
kept to herself and then died
on my father's birthday
his the only one in summer
when I was little
always disappointed he
never chose cake but
wanted apple pie
life's diversity giving
a first hint toward
divergences I didn't dream
existed then, people
going their separate ways
families scattering
across continents
time itself following
different calendars
as the Julian sundial in
the cathedral close
reminds me suggesting
days which didn't even exist
to be a birthday
eighteen years since
my father died
along with his shadows
his pain and
how he used to
get out his little key

check his box
long after the mail
had come 'in case
someone's slipped us
a hundred-dollar bill'

Sown

That ridge, fir trees, water
darkening

the house is empty, the house
which burned

once there was a woman
evil genius by her cradle

genes
no

(quarry water dark, ridge of firs):
the ghosts of unlove

they sowed, sow, have sown
grasshopper eggs, the ground of unlove

is a sieve of eggs
you walked on, walk on

have been walking on
locust eggs

(you didn't crave a leading role
you simply craved)

all is tense, even in death
you can't burn tense

you can only

beyond the ridge a house burned

what can you only

fir trees, quarry

Santa Catalina

The plain blurs
to sky as dusk descends.
I ride caught
in some time-bend

like old films,
walking in place
while the stage-set plays
its games with space –

until the horse balks,
ears flicking back
at a strange dark force
across our track.

I dismount, kneel, see
a tumbling stream
of half-inch-long frogs,
thrusting, teeming

toward the reed-bed
on my right hand.
A high bank left –
there's no way round.

In their millions
surging, spilling.
I feel cold. Each step
will be a killing.

A water bird
on the still lagoon
whistles once. Reeds stir
beneath a rim of moon.

After a Reading of *Poetry of the Greek Crisis*

I came upon the statues on the library steps,
still erect: the youth with folded wings,
feathered tips almost touching his ankles,
the three women – marble as any goddess.
The library closed as it has been since
the trouble began, and went on, and goes on –
no longer a crisis followed on international
news channels. No longer a nightmare
one would wake from, shaken by
the hideous vision, but already stepping
into the kitchen, reaching for the briki, coffee –

No, we won't wake. The kitchen is full of strangers,
there's no coffee, the library is closed,
and the winged lad's chipped plinth reads
. . . *bearer of souls*.

Mastic: One Ingredient

Tears bleed from cuts in the trunk.

Healing Cream the handwritten label promises.
I unscrew the lid, breathe in.
Honey too.

Mastic: a word encountered
seven lives ago in a surreal poem.

Resin oozes from lentisk bark.
Harvest of wounds.

I find the poem for the first time in years and read
lightning strikes thresh youth.

Thrash youth?

Almond oil. Hypericum.

Old scars we chew and chew.

Apology

They say that footprints don't go backward
but they forgot window-shopping and how
not pinned down by a weight of decision which
excludes so many other options footsteps can
return again and again to the tiny candle on
the doll-house-size welsh-dresser shelf in
an antique shop on Bleecker St parading too
an array of grandfather clocks tick-tocking all
at different hours which the young man named Carney
admires wanting us to get together in a house with
a grandfather clock in the living-room and maybe
that sofa would go? he turns to me dreaming but
I am dreaming of childhood and doll-houses
and once-upon-a-time in the days before
these questions still too great for me

The Thriving Magpie

I have seen magpies raiding gardens
and flapping up from roads in Italy and Norway,
from Holland to Tel Aviv. Now in England

as I make tea to *Tweet of the Day* one
is pecking among snowdrops, its tail-feathers
glistening greeny-purple in the early light.

Someone is talking about this bird he hates:
for its human failings, apparently – bully tactics,
raids on the weak, eye to the main chance.

But what about its intelligence and adaptability?
And what it sees in mirrors? The magpie's
singular capacity to recognise itself?

Quay

Rain sluices. The quay gleams.
Yesterday sea and air
felt one they were so clear.
Surely, we too could breathe

like fish, scour the sea-floor
among plant fronds, currents,
the weight of liquid salt. Then
through the skerries cloud poured.

Waves slap beneath the boards,
churn, smack. A fishing-boat
last night returned to port.
Now in an open shed

we see a man's bent back
and, flopped across scrubbed wood,
a halibut. Huge. Dead.
He saws, slab by white slab.

Quanta, USA

1

Four girls erupt from a phone booth
and move off down broad empty Main St
giggling and shrieking. The Post Office flag slumps limp.

Wide-screen America. The street lies in an envelope of heat,
prelude to a Western, ready for the cowboy
to swagger into town. Wind-screen America.

1956. Our ancient Chrysler beetles along.
Warm air pours through the open windows.
My parents spot a Howard Johnson's,

call an ice-cream stop. I gaze at the gleaming list.
28 Varieties. Mint-chocolate-chip? Coconut? Macaroon?
Vanilla? my father teases.

2

It was so hot here my brain was melting,
a friend writes on a postcard from Hannibal, Missouri.
How could Mark Twain come from those oppressive plains?

I'm reading my mail in the subway, still cool
from a swim. Think of Huck and Jim, and the Mississippi
with its cargo of dead negroes, cows and chicken coops.

My father's family left that area in a covered wagon.
Then got winter-blocked at another river – they survived
on cabbage. Not part of the mythology,

not pumpkin, which very colour is a promised land.
When my cousin talked of root-cellars, and all
they held, I saw pumpkins piled everywhere.

3

Forever, I notice in small letters on
a postage-stamp of the Liberty Bell. Forever cracked?
Like the sand-dollar from a California beach

which I don't throw away? Or something
more sombre in the promised Dream? The gun
tucked in a boot on a leg emerging from the black Mercedes

which blocks the street in Soho; a man in a dark suit
steps out, smooths down his ruckled cuff.
Laughs flash in shadowy doorways.

We celebrate the Bicentennial with Romanian friends –
they see no flaw in a land where finally
they feel free. There are flags everywhere.

4

Amazing grace, I think, studying a poster.
Dance Theater of Harlem: Josephine Baker and her perfect partner
moving into the fragile moment?

A friend's dancing daughter was dropped one evening
on her spine. These sudden sharp turns in the road –
and you wake up in a new bare place.

That startling freedom. My father laughed aloud
as he told how the Model T *just sailed through the air
into a stubble-field. I was six or seven.*

He was back from hospital, chatting from his wheel-chair
while I hung paintings. I'd asked, *what about
some* happy *childhood memory, Dad?*

5

Slowly sliding down and around the snail-spiral,
helter-skelter Guggenheim ramp, crowded as any Fun-Fair,
I think of Ralph, telling how of all of them,

and I know he's not the greatest, he felt
closest to Juan Gris – and me for the first time
seeing a lean cheek sliced in cubes and planes.

My mother-in-law, who prefers her portraits
real, is waiting for us in the forecourt.
Ever impulsive, she's bought us all ice-cream cones –

strawberry, lemon, mocha, pistachio.
We find her looking frantically toward the swing-door
between hasty licks at a Niagara of drips.

6

. . . the vast plains of the Guser Crater region.
I gaze at an image sent by NASA's rover-robot *Spirit*
after almost three years in a wilderness of space.

Mars is called *the geologic promised land.*
The mind can't really grasp it. The Mojave Desert?
Wyoming without sagebrush?

We see what we know, like the villagers
in Congo who said, when questioned, a film
on public health was about a hen.

The chalky fields, pale in moonlight, around the house
we moved to when we married felt alien:
earth was black, or crumbly-dark, or red.

7

Wet-headed, I climb the path from a lake
wide as a sea, walk three long blocks past mansions
with vast lawns, cross the tracks and turn

into the library, where I find a rest-room,
comb my hair. All scale has changed.
I am a child again, the world beating huge

and warm about me. A teacher's voice
echoes telling us we were *so lucky,*
no place on earth so blessed.

Main Street is one-storey, broad and empty.
The Post Office flag hangs limp in the still afternoon.
A poster proclaims this the *Queen of Suburbs.*

8

The train window looks out on silos, grain-elevators,
a large field where dark brown cattle range
near the tracks. We pass Rugby, North Dakota:

Geographical center of the North American continent.
As triangulated from where in 1931?
(And what of shrinking ice-caps, global melt?)

My mother's friend talked of *star-music*
in her log-cabin childhood not far from here, how
the Northern Lights swirled *in wheels and fountains.*

At the state-line time itself seizes another hour.
On a brief stop I stare at manikins in a shop-window,
the display of lingerie and dressy clothes.

9

The school-hall is jammed. People are up in arms about
a bill to give bison roaming-space. The spokesman flown in
from Washington looks lost and out-of-touch.

The next day we drive for hours – license-plates
boast the *Big Sky* – to an elk-reserve; watch a wandering male
cut stray does from another male's herd, then –

mock-scuff, antler-toss – lose them again.
Someone shows me his *new toy,* a palm-sized gun, *for snakes.*
Later we pass a bluff where dinosaurs were found.

The diner is short-staffed. Someone they all know off sick.
Plenty of time to ponder cornbread? hash-browns?
As we wait, the coffee never stops.

Orion

I'm dressing in the glow of Betelgeuse,
reach out a span of light years for a belt.
Heavenly King, still in my sky.
Your depth and drift a sea of comfort.
Waves hold my parents' faces to the light
before they break, and break again, tossing shells
gathered in Sahara sand, a fish splayed
through Alpine slate. Stories told
from once-upon-a-paleo-time,
which still is Now.
                  Present as the child
in an aged face beaming as she plucked
a dandelion-clock, and blew. That child
who loved Sirius because he was a dog,
and drew her hopscotch using chalk which
in its day breathed living bubbles into mud.

When my grandmother resurrects it's not

in a lift of white wings from a country churchyard not
in the garden where each flower had a name
nor even in the yellow canary-singing kitchen

but on the Greyhound Bus seated beside
a girl with chartreuse hair and blue cartoons
alarmingly tattooed on her little arm

Grandma always polite smiles at this apparition
but decides to try again and finds herself
in a queue for the same bus behind

a fellow with dreadlocks and one ear-ring
out of an old picture of hell chatting
to a girl in transparent bum-huggers –

not a word she had ever come across or
would have dreamed of using
if she had but here she is thinking it

and thinking the Greyhound Bus is the only
familiar thing this must be Oakland
maybe she hasn't resurrected after all

maybe this is the real death when now
you've been dead for a while you are ready
to resurrect to go back like after a holiday ready

for the first day of school with your new
pencil-box and special sharpener
and new crisp hair-ribbons –

and you can't it's not like that anymore
just strange little screens and parents telling teachers – teachers! –
it isn't good enough it isn't acceptable

is this the real death? she asks
my unresurrected Grandpa who is floating in a blue-grass sea
or the real resurrection into a place so new

that you discover you are new too? and the young man
in dreadlocks has the sweetest smile
smiling back for the freedom of it

Lucky the One who's Made the Voyage of Odysseus

G.S.

Yes, lucky indeed to have made that voyage, heard
the echo of his footsteps, stories of his struggles
and how he got on with them, like a saint
I don't have to worship for an impossible goodness
but a man who faced the next thing.
I imagine he's telling me how one goes on when
by whatever conjunction of choice and chance
the journey takes us through a dangerous strait,
or the bag of winds comes untied.

I speak for myself only, of course, and I know
I was lucky too in my boat, and the love
with which my parents rigged it. Theirs
was a great gift. Sometimes I imagine
even now they are travelling with me,
seated astern, out of the wind, in this vessel
they caulked with indissoluble glue, and that
thinking and thanking are a single breath.

I catch whispers on the wind, or when the sail
swings to a new tack, words in a language
we shared but has changed as the world
has changed. Words which like Proteus slip,
splash, hide in shifting expanding rings.
There are times these shoals of bubble-words
feel like the worst danger of all because we need them
even as they betray us, and how to grasp them
in such a way they reveal a true self?

Or it's the comrades – their oars turned
winnowing-fans – who betray not us but themselves.
Friends we have relied on, loved, join the lotus-eaters,
or in anger and bitterness fall overboard.
Then it's clear why Odysseus passed
through the underworld on his way home.
The dead are hard grain, all chaff
blown away on whatever prevailing wind.

Just the Two of Us

I long to take my desk on a naughty weekend,
just the two of us together to a rocky island with
a copse for kindling and starfish in the tide-pools,
whispering our small nothings away from the world.
Wood-burning stove, hot coffee, cosy duvet . . .
Rediscovering beneath three brochures,
old receipts, a pre-online bank statement,
dentist appointment, jotted shopping-list,
the scribbled bone of a poem.

Our retreat comes complete with a basket woven
of the sweet grass in Horse Heaven Country –
there's a feathered pattern picked out in
dark and lighter grasses which I'm reluctant to bury
under wastepaper, and note how strategically
the basket has been placed, next to the stove.

Hovering doubt arises when I read the bone-poem
on the back of its tattered envelope. Resuscitation
probably not advisable, even possible.
I glance into the stove, add a few sticks
and look at my desk with a question
in my eyes, remembering the days when
the sun fell across a fire-escape with pots
of petunias and basil and tomatoes
(I'd bought soil in a bag at Woolworths) –
fell in bars across an expanse where I wrote
around a sprawled grey cat. The poem
had its seed then, and maybe that's all
it was, a seed, like so many seeds
that fall to earth not to germinate, among
the prodigality of seeds in a prodigal universe.
The envelope is ragged, smudged.

I lay it aside, by the newspaper article
in a language hard to navigate now, and reach for
the bundle of letters stashed between
a business folder and the wall, old letters.
One is from my deceased mother's
103-year-old friend, with beautiful stamps on it,
of a woman chemist, and a sailing-ship –
the bundle lies there like a bowl of fruit while
I unfold a photocopy of a John Ashbery poem about
being trapped at a desk, and look up at my desk,
saying, *We never feel like that, do we? We're*
never trapped, and pull the duvet closer.

Patient

My husband pushes his bike
out of the gate leaning on it heavily
he has forgotten his cap
suffers from cold
I don't shout out the window
who wants to feel watched
he looks older than my grandfather
it's strange to see your husband
turn into the grandfather who
took his cap and stoop and a way
of moving with a wheelbarrow
out of your life so early
these are the thoughts
which balloon in the mind
how unsteady he seems
around the house too
is he going to fall
should I leap up
do it for him
remind him
what normal no longer is
the daily life
he took for granted
his accommodating body
energy
these are the poems
one can't write but
write themselves as I check
the Rayburn before he wakes
toss the last coal into the firebox
refill the hod bring in logs kindling

it's May but we're still
making an evening fire
take away the ashes
take away

The Hospital Café is Almost Empty

I take my coffee to a window table notice
how the pavement outside actually continues
the floor same level but in concrete this wall
was probably prefab just a thin skin
between me and out there just a small op but
the anaesthetic when we are young chopping wood
digging this is unimaginable someone else's life
poor chap and the sun shafts out there
making golden columns we can't imagine
being shut in a white room with the nurse
and her smiling explanations and her needle

MY AUNT AND ZBIGNIEW HERBERT

My Aunt and Zbigniew Herbert

i.m. Jane 1921-2006

1 *What Our Dead Do*

The will rejected any funeral
or memorial, categorically. Still
telling your father *I'll*
live without your love.

We would have dressed you
beautifully. We would
have argued about the clothes
shaking dust from

a plastic bag and drawing forth
a silk blouse you made in
the Fifties to say
And what about this one?

Into an oak coffin
we would have laid your silver
tear-drop, the little sail-boat
the purple blanket

from Northwestern, an inked
fish-print. We would
have lined it with letters, made
a burrow where you

could feel snug. A draught
of a letter recent as not long ago
reads *Dear Mr. Herndon,*
No one in this life

has given me so much, or
of such great value. Am I to go
to my grave not knowing
the error in the Chopin B♭ Prelude?

2 Farewell to the City

Colour-coded bags
hook onto the horseshoe sculpture
which stands in too much space
there is no piano

the space is threatening
not like when we sat with drinks by the rooster-lamp
looking over a city glowing in the night
there was a small red light high on a penthouse-mast for airplanes

The space was outside then

now it has come through the French windows
which are paint-chipped and rusting they don't close properly

the space is all around us
there is no piano

Horseshoe-nails stick out of the sculpture
where we hook the bags
which fill
they get heavy and sag

with bank statements holiday postcards news clippings
divorce documents recipes instructions
for assembling a tent
a letter

telling of a Sunday drive into New Mexico
you slid down hills of white sand it was so beautiful
you hardly noticed

the barbed wire and No Trespassing signs
around the Manhattan project

3 *Most Difficult is to Step Across the Abyss*
   Opening Beyond Your Fingernails

Never again
will a three-year-old sit
on a little stool
embroidering

and humming
her mother
is having a piano lesson
humming

and embroidering
in a world new
and wide
with fallen snow

Never again
in a vast white world
hear
the teacher say

that child
has perfect pitch
that child
should have lessons

The words
ring
over the opened abyss
all her life

even playing four hands
in the Anna Russell show
in New York City
the words lie

buried
like stones under snow
hard
ready to throw

4 *That is Why the World is Perfect*
   and Uninhabitable

It took a lot of energy
to create a perfect world

In all the chaos
finding the right shade
of purple
a seven-letter word for yellow

a complementary
sausage for kale

going down to the market at dawn
to search out a fish with scales firm enough fresh enough for
an ink-print of a perfect fish

Above all practising
getting it right
the technically precise dream in the ears
juxtaposed

with a vision of love
perfect technique
would draw love up from behind the horizon

it glowed you knew it was there

It was love which finally
would swell the music into a purple flower
with stamens
of gamboge

a word derived
from *Cambodia* where the pigment
comes from a gum-resin produced by trees of the genus Garcinia

you discovered in your huge dictionary
with a small surge of delight

the world an infinitesimal degree
more perfect

heavier

5 *He Valued Concrete Objects*
   Standing Quietly in Space

We keep finding
objects

a tiny stone head from Mexico
a silver tear-drop
a jade bead an arrowhead

each valued
in a larger pattern we can only perceive now
in its solution
and dissolution

a baby sand-dollar a round lidded-dish
stamped *Knole*

puzzle pieces
dropping into place

We don't want to find the last one
see it finished
taken away like the piano

leaving only an irregular space on the redwood bricks
which make the floor itself
into a quiet object

in the foreground of an empty city-scape
at dusk

Light from the rooster-lamp gleams on
the black-walnut coffee-table

where a bronze rabbi still floats in his bath
and a two-masted wooden sailboat
with wooden sails

leans into the breeze through
the open French windows

Cork coasters catch the tears
from our weeping drinks

6 Gentle Leibniz Who Called Music

a hidden
arithmetic
training
of the soul

lies
reincarnated in the next bed
your ward neighbour
who groans

and apologises
groans
and apologises
Sorry, darling

It's clear
that Mrs. Leibniz' groans
are an audible
manifestation

of her frustration
at the absence of music
in this new
training

music
gave glimpses
of a golden architecture catching the sun
between drifting clouds

In this new training
nothing
is hidden
not even the soul

under bare sky
arithmetic
has collided with mathematics
exponential subtraction

logarithms
exploding
beyond rhythms beyond patterns
of proportion

I know how she feels
you say
the soul in your eyes gleams a pinprick
of anger

7 In My Box Called the Imagination

In my box called the imagination
we are playing theatre
you and I

we've made a stage living-room with a piano
and a floor of redwood bricks

we are children
with all to play for
and as we are children
we begin arguing

I want the play to begin now

we aren't ready you protest
we have to get it right where are the doors for entrances
what characters are we going to play what will they be wearing
I want to wear the purple curtain you say
so what colour should the sofa be

I haven't thought about my costume at all
I dig into the box and find a pair of Robin Hood boots
and pull them on

what can Robin Hood do in a living-room you object

my answer is prompt
he shoots an arrow up through the open balcony windows
it rattles across the redwood floor and you see
that there's a silk thread attached
which you pull and pull and a rope comes up
he's going to rescue you from a wicked landlord

your eyes sparkle
you like that
but how can I get down a rope carrying things you ask
what about the piano

something will happen I assure you

but what you retort

8 *Fallen from the Whole*

It is this whole
now
which feels dangerous
the whole

visible
after an earthquake
concrete foundation
tilted awry

near an album
flung wide on three black-and-white photos
smiling

It is this whole now

when we lived in the present's
succession of
crippled moments

even insomnia felt
possible
we could dream
impatiently

even pain
we could dream

9 For Lack of a Nail the Kingdom has Fallen

No

for lack
of where to hammer the nail

for lack of that elusive
irreducible material
which can't shatter or melt when high-rises collapse

when palaces bridges streets crumple
shelves in mom-and-pop shops tilt at odd angles

We climb warily through rubble
looking for signs

a painting say
still hanging

on a nail fixed
into a panel which

no convolution
of earth or man
may rupture

a large abstract canvas
taut with black calligraphy

EDGELAND

Edgeland

Beyond the platform fence
the willows have put forth fuzzy
caterpillars. Milk-green leaf-shoots
thrust along the boughs.
A transparent pink in
the mottle below draws the eye
to a rabbit's ear; still
as still, back turned to early sun.

Spring sun refracts through glass
all the way to Gatwick. I sit
half-blinded. Is this
what I'll take with me? This glimpse
into the fullness on the margins of
any journey one may plan?

Once we returned to the magnolia
in fullest bloom. Its rapture
cast a pallor over our days away, effaced
the hill town, old piazza where
people sat with coffee,
easy pleasantries
dissolving in the steam.

Achaía

So many people fed us then.
So many strangers on trains broke off a chunk of bread,
crumbled cheese on it
and passed it to us
with a handful of dried figs.

Surely they were angels –
angels of God,
like in old tales.

In our sandals and innocent skin
we were children discovering a world of dew,
nothing to give in return beyond
our thanks, our wonder.

Those strangers long ago who invited us home
to tables in rooms up whitewashed steps –
was it food or words they gave us?
Salt. Birth. We remember
their woven blankets, the new sound
for *morning.*
Opening the shutters at dawn
as hill after hill unfolded in that first light, yes,
this was birth,
this was morning.

Pomegranates, Sky

Pomegranates blossom
in the window space.
The fresh joists smell of trees.
Banter. Hammer-blows.

The breeze wraps the house
close as vineyards, olive leaves.
Soon walls will show
grave wedding-photos,

a baby will be born, farm
receive new subsidies.
But for now sky
pours through the roofing-frame

like that grace which once
enfolded us when swallows laced
a bombed cathedral emptiness
and made it holy.

Will drudgery, drought,
crop-failure, grief drown
the promises that flow
so wide and free?

A wash of blue pours
over us, blessing
the young wife's bottle too.
She pours small glasses of rakí.

The Stag Melts into Leaf-Light

An apocryphal St Eustace sees the cross
caught in the stag's antlers, trusts his eyes as
my feet trust the branches of the pepper-tree,
my child-mind trusts Robin Hood was true.
Green fronds lace the air. Fuzzy nubs
of horn rise into limbs. I climb through dreams
which years on in a leafless wood – trunks
like iron bars, snow-silence on the valley-floor –
turn nightmare with a wracking thud.
I brake, get out. The huge body quivers once,
and sighs, becomes all stags forevermore.
His the antlers a small son will one day find,
whitening still over the chalet door.

Rest Stop

Drink black coffee from a thermos
sitting on a stump
                    - Gary Snyder

That lightness
pack just shed (body
                    on the verge of flight

        splashes of shade
            pool of sun

breath of chaparral –

curls of madrone bark stir in the breeze
more intricate
                    (tiny shadow movements
        more delicate
        than the curling peel of orange

a delicate insect hangs
                    suspended

Sheep, Swallows, Sparrowhawks

Vedi che si trasforma questo lembo
di terra solitaria in un crogiuolo - Montale

1

Room for us all, I say softly to the sheep
blocking the path, heads tucked between coarse clumps
of winter grass. *No need to move.* I slow my walk,
keep murmuring, but they shift while I pass,

raise their heads, gaze at me, diffident.
Young in a wide world. How to trust the new, what lies
beneath a voice? *Wool so white since the rain.*
I keep talking as I slip by down the steep descent,

boots, jeans spattered with chalky mud.
Once this place was new to me, soil so pale – unearthly
in eyes used to dark or red. Translating
to see fields spread grey as pearl.

2

The lopped trunks rose in a giant assemblage
of dead colossi. They milled around the church
like souls unable to reach out, or even whisper:
dismembered, crippled, un-made, come to nought.

Carnage. I stood appalled. No leaf-breath, rustle.
No frond for robin, blackbird, coal-tit, wren.
Naked bark. How many years ago was that?
Like seeing broken statues in a still park.

Yet here a mass of slender boughs is fanning
thick with leaf, pushing forth in frills, ruffles, darts –
green life irrepressible. Arms in thousands
held aloft. Outburst of an undead heart.

3

The dark at the edge of the box of light is a relief.
We don't have to look, can focus on John Hurt
peering side-stage into what isn't there
before he seats himself beneath the yellow bulb.

I think of the bundle of rags in her chair
who was my neighbour, the night she spent
failing to get a leg into the second knicker-hole.
At 6 a.m. she gave up. *I'd shot my bolt.*

What tape would she choose? Krapp's banana droops.
He rewinds. Listens. Despite the gall
of life, the crap under the yellow bulb, there are
moments – they move him, move in him still.

4

I'm walking home from the Village Hall, forgot
my torch again but there's a moon, climbing higher
now above a sleeping down. It silhouettes
a lace of twigs, then slips behind thin cloud

and rushes out again. The world turns that fast!
Hurrying us along a surface splashed and pleated
in strange transparencies and then, where the street
dips and bends, abruptly black, pitch-black.

Blind as a pilgrim in a dark wood, I'm faring
on faith. I know the copse will end, sky appear.
Each kicked pebble brings me nearer open road
again, house-windows lit, scattered stars.

5

Many of the portraits seem like photos
out of childhood, half-known, seen the way
one sees one's parents' friends – now come alive,
light playing tone-poems on their canvas skin,

patching *The Old Gardener* into the shade
he's resting in. I will the *Painter's Father*
to look up from his paper, catch my eye.
He loved you, I want to say, no one more.

Fingering ear-rings my father gave me
decades before, in the shop I stare at ghosts.
Page through the catalogue but know it's not
an aide-memoire I'm really looking for.

6

We'd been going over old texts she'd translated,
this spinster of an older school, when she
broke off, stood up with sudden urgency.
Come see my goldenrod! She fairly thrust me

into the unkempt space out back. Past
the bins and dead grass poking up through cracks
in old cement, the scrubby waste was washed
with gold – and she too gilded, standing there,

glimpsing again with child eyes a first world
bursting on her which she couldn't wait to share.
Chinks in time. *Look! Look!* I hear my own voice
tug Grandma from her cooking out the door.

7

He rests his spade, inhales. The smell of earth
runs through him to his boots. Clear as words
a blackbird calls: *What I do is me: for that I came.*
The blessing of it – beyond doubt: just to be

a part of things. Yesterday a sparrow-hawk
dropped like a bolt on a collar-dove. Right there,
while he was sitting on his stump. This intimacy
beyond love swelling through the years.

He's bled into this patch of land (all nettles once),
bound up cuts and gone back to digging.
Now swallows line the wires, soon away: they of the kind
that goes, he – rooted to a breath – that stays.

Romney Marsh

Stone floats. Churches are built on water.
Nave arches tilt wide a path toward
light coarse as wool, or fodder.
Here is faith in every property of matter.

This quiet hill was always dear to me
G.L.

Each time I take the back road home, I ponder
a slant of earth which gives the eye a constant
learned in childhood half a world away –
the walk home then lay straight up a steep hill.

Not that home is always safe, does not contain
complexities to choke the heart and blind
the fumbling mind. It is the hill itself
which reassures, a shoulder, there: that line

of down emerging from its cloud, the weight
and poise of it – and our right movement now.
We hurtle through the rush and tug of cross-winds,
unswerving as a leopard on the spring.

No Access

My father once dog-sat for a short stint
in leafy Princeton. I took a couple of nights
off from waitressing to trespass on academia,
a once-familiar world grown strange.
Strange as the visit back to Berkeley –
that day of life once green as foliage.
I walked across the campus and all
the faces scurrying were young. Like
looking in on your old backyard and not
recognising the creek, forget-me-nots.
Compare and contrast: the heave and surge
of beery bodies in a *White Horse* fug.
The lhasa apsos snubbed me with their snob name.
And Dad on the wagon. We drank lemonade.

Berkeley #5

I spent the afternoon looking around
the exhibition, standing my eyes inside the frame,
and then stepping back. The cold of poured concrete
leaked up through the floor in one painting.
You grow up in a certain place at a certain time,
and there can be an ache in what you recognise,
the same double-doors to the painter's studio
I clanged open leaving school, my father's
battered ashtray on his table. The squiggles
in *Berkeley #5* are not a map, just what
the body knew beyond all Berkeley fog,
a blind orientation climbing the hill home.
Never thinking of the geography that daily walk
took in, or how land might weigh in an artist's regard,
shapes of movement get encoded in one's bones.
All here in an angle, a jiggled line.
How many ways there were home.

Racing, Fathers

Racing down Endell St, over Long Acre
into Bow, threading the drifting clusters
of humanity which clog the pavement
on this gift of an evening in mid-May;
dodging a taxi spewing forth more bodies
to swell the crowd outside *The Lion King*,
and leaping across the Strand on two red lights
ahead of hurtling double-deckers, I gulp
another breath, river-scented now, and pant past
three languages and two photographers.
In the far lane a bicycle-taxi sails by –
wheels freer than wings (think Jacques Tati) –
and why couldn't my ticket have been taken
by a son whose awareness of the whole
beyond the weave of sound would infuse
a replay later with his father:
How did he get that spiritual quality
into a six-beat measure? I've never heard
the C Sharp Minor given a sense of brooding.
Racing slower now, I see the Festival Hall
lies closer to the bridge than I remembered.
Really, there's time (the light on the river
is water-coloured at this hour) – but then
the bell is pinging and I panic
again, rush blindly up to Level Four, Green Side
or not, filter, don't-quite-push, pause
at the door, and peer near-sightedly,
until *There he is*, I slide into the seat
next to my husband, grin *Hi*,
and cheeks burning, heart pounding
reach for the programme: still in time –
as every seat in the concert-hall
fills like small squares in a game
on the verge of completion – to register

Chopin, who's Medtner? Stravinski.
Yevgeni Kissin walks with due purpose
across the stage, bows, seats himself
at the keyboard and positions fingers
which on exactly the right beat set off
running, running, free as a bicycle-taxi
sailing across Waterloo Bridge . . .

During *Petrushka*, as the right hand takes
an oh, so light dash past the jarring,
jolting left, a tension of textures
accumulates, shoots off at angles.
I see my father painting jagged black strokes
onto the canvas later entitled with characteristic wit
Nude Rejects Black Swan.
I wish I could ring, hear his chuckle.
I wish he weren't dead.
He loved Stravinski.

The Migratory Birds

The houses I had they took away from me. The times
happened to be unpropitious: war, destruction, exile;
sometimes the hunter hits the migratory birds,
sometimes he doesn't hit them. Hunting
was good in my time, many felt the pellet;
the rest circle aimlessly or go mad in the shelters.

Seferis, 1946

1

No unholy visions set our screens on fire.
My parents were young in California then,
far away from war, Armageddon squeezed –

black-and-white, a flicker of images –
between the feature film and the cartoon.
The immigrants who came to rest on that

last edge found jobs of a kind, often made good.
We had little idea of their past.
Now their stories lap all our shores, unroll

before our eyes: brought near, made our stories too.
Uncomfortable at times as a chill draught
from a window we never knew could open.

2

Often on the beach you'll find piles of wet clothes:
migrants with nothing, dropped off-shore to swim
the river Jordan – or last loop of the Styx?

74

The sand beneath their feet as they emerged
was electric with all they could not fathom.
The sea lapped, blinding in dawn's early light.

They melt into towns where the faces
coming toward them in the street seem pale,
unsubstantial as the underworld shades

they will become. Spreading out bright cloths
and selling trinkets, beads. Below eye-level.
Not there, circling aimlessly, blown leaves.

3

The rubber dinghy, capacity eight,
could barely keep afloat under forty-three.
Many of them children. *You can't go back.*

The smugglers had forced them on at gunpoint.
People were bailing with broken bottles.
I just kept on steering, praying we'd see land.

You wonder how many have had to pass through
the underworld to get to where they are now –
and how many have stayed there. Shouts and cries

came over the waves from their sister dinghy.
There was nothing they could do – *we saw it sink.*
The one shall be taken, the other left.

Stoker

for Wendy, and long conversations

The clerk in the tourist shop in the middle
of a hot nowhere the bus stopped
was fervent: whatever that was good here,
whatever that was great came from Serbia.
It was Serbians who carried this motley nation forward
on their strong backs, Serbians who merited praise.
I saw carved wooden paper-knives for sale
like the one given me so long ago. None
of the letters I'd opened over the years
had come from the horse's mouth,
so to speak. This message was the first.
When war broke out in the then Yugoslavia,
it was no surprise. I even knew
the young man who had lit the fuse.

Silver

On the morning I was leaving for
the train across the prairies my paternal ancestors
knew from a covered wagon,

I put on the beaten silver ear-rings
my father, always random about his gifts,
gave me one July when I was still camping

in the studio, sleeping on the couch partitioned off
from three nudes – canvasses which might
have shocked a wagon-train

better maybe at survival than life
to judge from the love my grandparents didn't
know how to give their children.

Happy Birthday! he said
(I was born in March) tilting
two little half-hoops from his palm to mine.

He'd discovered love in a thumbnail reproduction
of Rosa Bonheur's *Horse Traders*,
couldn't stop looking,

loved it with his whole ten-year-old being,
spent his life searching each fresh canvas
to the depths of its horizon.

Your Holiness, Your Grace, Dear Sir, Dear Pope,

Were you the priest
who decades ago
opened the door
to a sailors' hostel
in Buenos Aires when
hopelessly at sea
I knocked around midnight?

I'd asked a passer-by
for a small hotel.
We swam through
a dark space toward a small table
where you placed your torch
between us, and asked
just what was I doing?

How improbable
that this may have been you –
but who can I thank for
the right words between us?
Was this old ballroom
the closest to a confessional
I have ever been?

Something was changed,
the way the dusty street
to the bus-station
the next morning
was charged and changed
by a lift of yellow petals
on the warm breeze.

Herald

She would fly in from Buenos Aires talking
of Titian, how the cross cut the canvas
in diagonals, talking of books, their farm,

her husband's Alzheimer's, and death
coming on his white horse. You wouldn't think
an angel would mention stomach troubles,

stop taking wine but I put it out of mind –
after all, angels can do what they like, even
complain about a hotel room on Jermyn Street,

and then we were talking again – about Cortázar,
her pilgrimage to his grave in Montparnasse,
his poem *Black Ten*, which begins

in the black of Nothingness.
When her daughter rang to say she'd died, I knew,
yes, black was the colour of Silence too.

Reminded

1

I idly thumb through
an old notebook as I wait
for a bed in the cardiac ward.

Waiting for the ferry.
My heart has missed some boat,
is standing there waving a bit wildly.

Forced to see this beautiful place,
be here, instead of just passing through.
Yes, being here.

How beautiful it is.

2

> *Masks in the Arctic were never intended*
> *to disguise – rather to reveal an inner truth.*

Cicada, Pickpocket, The Faithful Fiancée,
Twin, Bald One . . . . Death
in Spanish dresses in a thousand guises.

Think of the sugar skulls
in Mexico iced with your name.
Clothes are a kind of transparency,

hospital gown flapping open
at the back. Screens
revealing inner truths,

the leaky valve, unruly heart.

Variation on a Theme by Montale

Moss is creeping back to this scrag-end
of railway-land. The inch of water which froze
in lamina has thawed. A ruddy stem
entangled through the thicket
signals a choked rose.
Spring's slow onset
in this fringe.

Bells clang, and the train draws up.
As I turn toward the beeping door, a trick of light
shifts my gaze higher: dove-soft buds
exploding on each willow-tip
flicker past the eye
and the eye clinging still
a mile down the rail.

The miracle which takes place one day
will be a miracle of timing: precise
as music given its full measure.
We won't emerge from a late train only
longing to get home,
too weary for
the nightingale in
the station carpark singing.

Quasimodo at Dawn

This morning I took my neighbour's dogs
for an early walk thinking how aged seven
or eight I'd awake into the summer dawn
and leap out of bed towards a lark of a day,

grabbing a peach as I crept out the door.
Running down Euclid onto the campus
and across the creek where we built dams
at the foot of a lawn sloping down from a building

I learned twenty years later to call Ag Econ
when a friend from Sicily was studying there –
it was he who gave me a book of Quasimodo:
We're each alone on the heart of the earth . . .

Running into the quiet light in the joy
of the morning *pierced by a ray of sun,*
like Jan's little dogs bursting with the delight of it,
no inkling how *suddenly evening falls.*

About the Author

Margaret Wilmot was born in Berkeley, where she also studied at the University of California. She then worked as a TEFL teacher in the Mediterranean and New York before marrying and moving to Sussex in 1978. Her work has appeared in various British poetry publications including *Acumen, Artemis, Assent, Cinnamon, Frogmore, Magma, Oxford Poetry, Nottingham, Rialto, Scintilla, Smiths Knoll, Staple, Temenos* and *The North*. In 2013 Smiths Knoll published *Sweet Coffee*, her debut pamphlet.

Acknowledgements

Thanks are due to the editors of the following in which some of the poems have previously appeared *Poetry South East, Artemis, Scintilla, Not in the Plan* (Carers' Anthology, 2017), *From Belize to Havana* (Biscuit Publishing, 2002), *The Frogmore Papers, Acumen, Crux*.

THE HIGH WINDOW

The following collections of poetry are also available directly from our website:
https://thehighwindowpress.com/the-press/

A Slow Blues, New and Selected Poems by David Cooke
Angles & Visions by Anthony Costello
The Emigrant's Farewell by James W. Wood
Four American Poets edited by Anthony Costello
Dust by Bethany W. Pope
From Inside by Anthony Howell
The Edge of Seeing by John Duffy
End Phrase by Mario Susko
Bloody, proud and murderous men, adulterers and enemies of God
by Steve Ely
Bare Bones by Norton Hodges
Wounded Light by James Russell
Bone Antler Stone by Tim Miller
Wardrobe Blues for a Japanese Lady by Alan Price;
Trodden Before by Patricia McCarthy
Janky Tuk Tuks by Wendy Holborow
Cradle of Bones by Frances Sackett
Of Course, the Yellow Cab by Ken Champion
Forms of Exile: Selected Poems of Marina Tsvetaeva
trans. by Belinda Cooke
West South North North South East by Daniel Bennett
Surfaces by Michael Lesher
Songs of Realisation by Anthony Howell